BIPOLAR DISORDER COMPLETE GUIDE

Comprehensive Strategies to Understanding, Supporting, And Managing the Challenges of Loving Someone by Effectively Overcoming their Conditions and Symptoms

Dr. Jude Nathan

Copyright ©

Contents

Introduction

Welcome to the "Bipolar Disorder Complete Guide". Living with bipolar disorder can feel like being on an emotional roller coaster, with dizzying highs and shattering lows. This book is intended to be your reliable guide through the stormy journey of bipolar disorder, providing practical advice, caring support, and expert insights to help you manage every twist and turn. Bipolar disorder is a complicated and frequently misunderstood condition that affects millions of individuals worldwide. Understanding the complexities of bipolar disorder is critical, whether you have recently been diagnosed, have been living with the disorder for years, or are caring for a loved one.

This book seeks to demystify the disorder by offering plain and understandable information about its causes, symptoms, and treatments. These pages contain a variety of information on themes such as recognizing the symptoms of bipolar disease, comprehending its impact on children, and determining the differences between youth bipolar and Asperger's syndrome. You'll also learn about the significance of accurate diagnosis, the efficacy of various therapies, and practical ways of dealing with the disease in everyday life.

The Bipolar Disease Complete Guide goes beyond the medical and psychological components of bipolar disease to explore the human and emotional dimensions of living with it. We talk about how to love and support someone with bipolar disease, how to achieve success despite obstacles, and the need for self-care and mental health maintenance. This book is intended for people who have been diagnosed with bipolar disorder, as well as their family, friends, and careers.

It is a complete resource that promotes comprehension, empathy, and resilience. By the end of this book, you will have the tools and knowledge to confront bipolar disorder head-on, with hope and confidence that it can be effectively managed.

Join us on this journey to better understand bipolar disorder and learn ways to restore stability, joy, and a feeling of normalcy in your life. Your trip to overcoming bipolar begins here.

Order a copy for yourself and your loved ones...

Description

Are you or someone you love suffering from bipolar disorder? You are not alone; this book is an essential companion on your path to stability and well-being. "Bipolar Disorder Complete Guide" teaches you all you need to know, from the fundamentals to long-term management. Imagine a life in which your emotional highs and lows are more than just mood swings; they are tremendous forces that impact every area of your life. "The Bipolar Disorder Complete Guide" is here to help you navigate the complexities of this challenging condition. This book also provides clear, compassionate insights on bipolar disorder, as well as practical advice and effective ways to assist you or your loved ones in managing the disorder's impact on everyday life.

Key topics covered in this book:

Introduction to Bipolar Disorder:
Learn about bipolar disorder and why it's critical to obtain the correct treatment. Understanding Bipolar Disorder to Get Help: Gain a thorough understanding of the nature of this disorder to seek and accept treatment.

Causes of Bipolar Disorder: 7 Things to Know:
Learn about the significant variables that lead to the development of bipolar disorder.

Why People Fail Treatment:
Learn about typical traps and how to prevent them.

How to Recognize Bipolar Symptoms and Their Importance:
Determine the crucial signs and why they are important.

Five Important Symptoms and Signs of Bipolar Disorder You Shouldn't Ignore: Discover the key indicators that require quick action.

Some Bipolar Disorder Warning Symptoms:
Be aware of the early warning signals so that you can take preventative action.

What to Do If Diagnosed with Bipolar Disorder:
Actionable things to take following a diagnosis to guarantee the best possible outcomes.

How to Manage Bipolar Disorder Without Complications:
Effective ways for maintaining a balanced existence.

What You Should Know and Do About Your Child's Bipolar Disorder:
Tips for parents to help their children deal with this disorder.

Common Bipolar Disorder Symptoms in Children:

Recognize and address symptoms in young people.

Bipolar Disorder Therapy Options for Children:
Discover the many therapy options for children.

Long-Term Bipolar Disorder Treatment:
Tips for managing bipolar disorder in the long run.

How to Be Successful Despite Bipolar:
Techniques for achieving personal and professional success while managing bipolar disorder.

Medications for Bipolar Disorder and Usage:
Comprehensive information on pharmaceuticals and their proper application.

How to Treat Bipolar Disorder with CBT:
Use Cognitive Behavioural Therapy as an effective therapy option.

And so much more...

"Bipolar Disorder Complete Guide" is a lifeline for everyone dealing with bipolar disorder. With practical counsel, expert insights, and sincere encouragement, this book teaches you how to take control and live a whole life despite the difficulties of bipolar disease. Take the first step towards understanding and managing this condition with confidence and compassion. Order a copy for yourself or a loved one.

Chapter 1

Introduction to Bipolar Disorder

Bipolar disorder is a mental condition that produces extraordinary changes in a person's mood, energy, activity level and focus. It was originally known as manic-depressive sickness or manic depression. Daily duties may be difficult to do during these transitions.

Types of Bipolar Disorder

Bipolar disorder comes in three Major forms. Clear changes in mood, energy, and activity levels are present in all three categories. These moods range from highly "down," sad, indifferent, or hopeless periods (known as depressive episodes), to excessively "up," euphoric, irritated, or energizing behavior. Hypomanic episodes are less intense manic episodes.

- **Bipolar I disorder**:
is characterized by manic symptoms that are severe enough to require immediate medical attention or by manic episodes that persist for at least seven days (almost every day for the majority of the day).

Depressive episodes frequently happen too, lasting at least two weeks. A mixed episode of depression is one in which a person has both manic and depressive symptoms at the same time. "Rapid cycling" refers to the occurrence of four or more manic or depressive episodes in a calendar year.

- **Bipolar II disorder**:
is characterized by a sequence of hypomanic and depressed episodes. In bipolar I disorder, the hypomanic episodes are less severe than the manic episodes.

- **Cyclothymic disorder (also called cyclothymia):**
Is characterized by recurrent hypomanic and depressive symptoms that do not meet the criteria for hypomanic or depressive episodes due to their lack of intensity or duration. Bipolar illness symptoms that do not fall into one of the three categories above are occasionally referred to as "other specified and unspecified bipolar and related disorders."

Often, bipolar disorder is discovered in the late adolescent or early adult years. Bipolar symptoms can occasionally manifest in young people. Bipolar disorder typically necessitates lifetime therapy, even though the symptoms can change over time. People can better their quality of life and control their symptoms by adhering to a prescribed treatment plan.

Symptoms and Signs of Bipolar Disorder

People who have bipolar disorder go through moments of exceptionally high emotion, modify their sleep and activity schedules, and exhibit out-of-character behaviors, frequently without being aware of the potential negative consequences. Episodes of mood are these unique times. A person's mood episodes differ greatly from their regular moods and behaviors. The symptoms last every day for the majority of the day throughout an episode. Additionally, episodes might linger for several days or even weeks.

Symptoms of a Manic Episode:

- Feeling incredibly pleased, elevated, agitated, or touchy
- Feeling energized or jittery and being more energetic than normal
- having less of a need to sleep

- speaking quickly and about a variety of subjects (a "flight of ideas")
- Flustered thinking
- having the capacity to multitask without becoming exhausted
- a high desire for eating, alcohol, sex, or other enjoyable pursuits
- having an exceptional sense of importance, talent, or strength.

Symptoms of a Depressive Episode:

- Feeling extremely depressed, unhappy, or worried
- being sluggish or restless
- sleep too much, wake up too early, or have difficulties getting asleep
- speaking very slowly, feeling as though they have nothing to say, or frequently forgetting things
- difficulty focusing or making decisions
- feeling incapable of performing even basic tasks
- being uninterested in nearly all activities
- Feeling useless or forlorn, or contemplating suicide or death

An episode with mixed features occurs when a person has both manic and depressed symptoms at the same time. People may experience tremendous sadness, emptiness, or hopelessness as well as extreme vigor during an episode with mixed features.

Even if a person's symptoms are less severe, they still can have bipolar disorder. For instance, hypomania, a milder version of mania, is experienced by some people with bipolar II disease.
A person experiencing a hypomanic episode could feel excellent, be productive, and carry on with daily activities.

Even though the person may not feel anything is wrong, family members and friends may notice changes in the person's mood or level of activity as potential bipolar disorder symptoms. Hypomanic individuals risk developing severe mania or depression if untreated.

Diagnosis of Bipolar Disorder

People with bipolar disorder can have healthy, busy lives with the proper diagnosis and treatment. The initial step is to consult with a healthcare professional. To rule out additional potential causes, the medical professional might do a physical examination and other required medical testing.

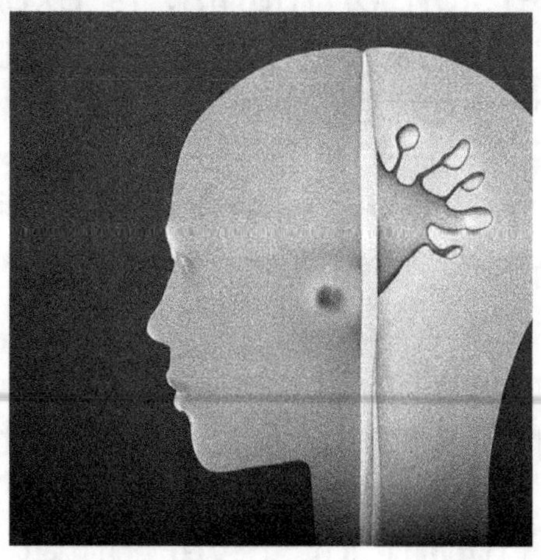

The health care practitioner may then carry out a mental health examination or refer a patient to a mental health professional who has received training in diagnosing and treating bipolar illness, such as a psychiatrist, psychologist, or clinical social worker.

Bipolar disorder is typically diagnosed by mental health professionals based on a patient's symptoms, lifetime experiences, history, and, in certain circumstances, family history. Youth diagnostic accuracy is particularly crucial.

Bipolar Disorder and Other Conditions

Anxiety disorders, attention-deficit/hyperactivity disorder (ADHD), drug or alcohol abuse, or eating disorders are common co-occurring problems in patients with bipolar disorder. There are times when severe manic or depressive episodes are accompanied by psychotic symptoms, such as hallucinations or delusions.

The individual's heightened mood often corresponds with psychotic symptoms. For instance, a person experiencing psychotic symptoms during a depressive episode might believe they are financially wrecked, whereas a person experiencing psychotic symptoms during a manic episode can think they are well-known or possess extraordinary abilities. A doctor can assess whether a patient has bipolar disorder or another disorder by looking at the patient's symptoms throughout the illness and their family history.

Risk Factors Associated with Bipolar Disorder include

Bipolar disorder's potential causes are being researched. Most people concur that a person's likelihood of developing the illness is likely to be influenced by a wide range of circumstances. According to certain research, people with bipolar disorder have different brain structures and functions from those who do not have the condition or any other mental illness. Scientists may be better able to comprehend bipolar disease and choose the most effective therapies if they have a better treatment understanding of these brain distinctions. Currently, rather than using brain imaging or other diagnostic procedures, healthcare professionals base a patient's diagnosis and strategy on their symptoms and medical history.

- Genetics

According to some studies, some persons are genetically predisposed to bipolar disorder. According to research, individuals who have a parent or sibling who has bipolar disorder are more likely to have the condition themselves. No one gene is responsible for the illness; several genes are involved. Researchers may be able to create novel medicines by learning more about the function that genes play in bipolar disease.

Chapter 2

Understanding Bipolar Disorder to Get Help

Most bipolar sufferers have a single objective. To lead a life that is as typical as possible is the aim. You may also want to be able to enjoy your daughter's graduation, get through the day without any emotional problems, and get through the important meeting at work without anyone wondering what's wrong with you. You must thoroughly comprehend your condition before you can truly learn to manage your bipolar disorder. To the best of your ability, you must be aware of what occurs so that you can put your coping strategies into action. There is no way to prevent these things from happening to you with absolute certainty. However, there are a ton of skills you can pick up to assist you change your perspective. To help you comprehend what is happening to you, we will first provide you with all the information you require on your condition. If you are a family member who merely wants to assist a person who has bipolar disorder, by all means, you may also get the knowledge required to provide the assistance that you can do. Extremes in mood and sensations are a symptom of bipolar disorder.

Without a doubt, persons who have bipolar disorder have serious and incapacitating symptoms. It is a mental illness, and therapy is important. You may have heard bipolar disorder referred to as manic depression or that someone with it has a manic-depressive disorder. Scientists have discovered that manic behavior is just one extreme of this illness, though. The depression component is the other portion of it. Both of these ailments must be treated because they are quite significant for your health and even your life span.

Although there is no known etiology for bipolar disorder, researchers are striving to identify one. In addition, you may be certain that numerous researchers are working to find a treatment for the illness. But in the interim, it's important to consider what we already know about bipolar disorder and how it affects the person you are.

Most patients with bipolar disorder first experience symptoms in their early teens. Some people think that puberty is what causes it. Others won't experience this disease till they are just beginning their adult lives. Your lifetime can also be affected by bipolar. Bipolar disorder is, for the majority of people, a condition that doesn't always exist.

You don't constantly encounter mood swings or other types of experiences that come and go in a matter of seconds. Some people, for instance, experience spells that linger for several weeks. Others will possess them for a short while.

Although having bipolar can cause your symptoms to worsen all the time, this is a very uncommon occurrence. If you don't seek bipolar treatment, your condition will probably keep getting worse. Without a doubt, depression itself is fatal. So, choosing not to seek assistance is not an option. The good news is that you may manage your disease and lessen your symptoms with the use of drugs, treatments, and therapies.

Chapter 3

Causes of Bipolar Disorder 7 Things to Know

eing intelligent and in good health is necessary for success in life. The central processing unit of our body, the brain, must be flawless or us to have a happy and successful life, although any physical limitations of the body can be overcome. We need a sharp mind for all of our errands to comprehend our surroundings, act quickly, and make well-considered decisions. We also need to have control over our emotions in addition to a brain that functions correctly. Being excessively happy or furious all the time would not be of any benefit to us. To use the proper phrase, all of our psychological components must be sufficiently balanced.

What happens if you find out that you or someone you know has a brain disorder? Bipolar disorder is one of these widespread brain disorders. In severe circumstances, this illness can cause suicides in addition to having an impact on our emotions and daily actions.

1. There are numerous contributing factors to bipolar disorder. Similar to how different fibers come together to weave a textile, demands from our family, friends, and jobs combine to cause this illness.

2. According to medical professionals, having a blood family with bipolar disorder does not necessarily guarantee that you will also have this condition, but it does raise your risk. Similarly to this, the absence of a family history of the condition does not guarantee that you won't develop it.

3. Overall, luck is the secret to recovering from any illness or sickness.

4. Cyclical mood fluctuations, whether they start in adolescence or later in life, can be used to describe bipolar illness. There have also been several instances when bipolar disorder has affected young children.

5. This illness does not discriminate against anyone based on their social class, race, or ethnicity.

6. Medical professionals combine antidepressants, mood stabilizers, anti-psychotics, or anti-maniacs with psychotherapy to treat bipolar disorder.

7. Patients with bipolar disorder share certain common biologic features. The tests and imaging scans can be used to demonstrate these. Such individuals have elevated levels of the stress hormone cortisol, as well as hyperactivity that manifests as atypical movements and emotional functions above and beyond normal behavior.

Reduced brain activity in some ways is related to cognitive function, a quick biological clock (which controls our body's circadian rhythm, specifically the cycle of walking and sleep), and significant calcium overload in the brain cells.

While these were some overarching and fundamental features regarding the bipolar disease, experts have categorized its fundamental components as follows:

- Biologically or biochemically
- Genetic or family
- Medication
- Environmental

- Biologically or biochemically

Regarding the biochemical components, the specialists say that bipolar disorder manifests in a specific region of the brain when several neurotransmitters, or chemical messengers, go awry. Dopamine, serotonin, norepinephrine, and other neurotransmitters may all have a role in the bipolar disorder that is currently occurring. In these situations, the illness might lie latent or sleeping in our brains for years before being awakened by stress or other external triggers. The brain of a patient with bipolar disorder is wired differently than the brain of a healthy person, according to medical experts. This also explains the excruciating changes in the strong emotions.

- Genetic or Family

Such people can undoubtedly get bipolar disorder if they have a first-degree blood family who has the illness. In this situation, the first-degree blood relatives could be parents, siblings, or children. Anyone can fall victim to this condition, even though this simply raises the risk in comparison to those who have a similar familial background. The search for the specific genes that cause this condition is a top priority for research professionals.

- Medication

Bipolar disorder may be brought on if a patient receives the wrong diagnosis and drugs that are unable to control the condition or worsen it. Sometimes a doctor or psychiatrist will just diagnose a patient with depression without noticing any other strange changes in the patient that might be leading them astray from the initial diagnosis.

This may result in the wrong medication being prescribed. For instance, if a patient is susceptible to bipolar disorder, an anti-depressant prescription may cause a manic episode. It occurs when a misdiagnosis causes the manic stage to be missed. Anti-manic & antidepressant drugs are administered together to bipolar illness patients. The anti-manic drugs essentially create a barrier to guard your patient against mania, which is triggered by the anti-depressants they are taking. Numerous more medications, in addition to those already mentioned, can cause bipolar illness in people.

These include over-consumption of caffeine, designer drugs (such as cocaine, amphetamines, etc.), corticosteroids, appetite suppressants, and medications for colds. All of these result in madness. Bipolar disorder is also brought on by the misuse of alcohol and other stimulants.

- Environmental

The stressful life of the current era might also be a factor in this mood illness. In our daily lives, when we are concerned with all of our social, professional, and personal ties, countless events could occur, including career loss, shocking loved one death, relocations, pregnancies, financial bankruptcies, etc. Bipolar disorder-causing stress can affect people of all ages and health conditions, including old adults, adolescents, pregnant women, etc. There are significant changes that people go through in all of these ages and circumstances, and those who have a fragile family foundation or are dealing with low self-esteem are more likely to have a crisis.

According to the specialists, all it takes is one single trigger for the condition to manifest, at which point the cycles start. It may be difficult to control the condition if it is not identified early enough. However, those who have a high sense of self-awareness, coping skills, and defense mechanisms can handle the circumstance very successfully.

Chapter 4

Why You Should Seek Help

A mental illness is bipolar. It is unlike a cold, which will pass. It is not similar to a broken leg, which will naturally recover. Bipolar can worsen if a specialist is not consulted. It is impossible to predict whether your health will become worse slowly or at all. However, evidence indicates that those who do not seek treatment for their disease will experience consequences for both themselves and their families. Additional medical issues can exacerbate bipolar if you already have it. Bipolar disorder, for instance, will make it difficult for you to manage your anxiety.

This can be a very serious issue when it poses a threat to your life, such as when you have an alcohol addiction. Your life may be in danger if you are unable to quit drinking. Your health will suffer from the drinking, and bipolar disorder can cause you to think erratically and put yourself in risky circumstances. This makes asking for assistance imperative.

Some people may have very little time between depression symptoms and manic symptoms. Rapid switching between symptoms could confuse and potentially cause health concerns. You will have a lot of trouble just because of this quick cycling. Even worse outcomes are possible. Unbelievably, it is conceivable to experience both mania and despair simultaneously. Your mind and emotions become entangled with one another as a result of this. You're upset and irritated.

You are not able to eat or sleep. Your thoughts won't order themselves. Even worse, people are more prone to consider suicide when this occurs. Because they are not thinking logically at all, people in this state can make bad decisions, which can be highly dangerous. There is also the issue of psychosis. Psychosis can result from bipolar symptoms that include both manic and depressive symptoms. Your personality is jumbled as a result of this extremely terrible mental condition. You lack a perception of what is genuine and what is false. You are delusional and experiencing hallucinations.

Even people who have a strong sense of conviction sometimes choose to go in a different direction. Beyond the medical risks that living with bipolar illness exposes you to, it also has catastrophic repercussions on your relationships. Many bipolar individuals will struggle to maintain relationships. Due to the mood swings they experience, they could switch from one individual to the next swiftly. Additionally, people with bipolar disorder frequently misjudge how to interact with others. They merely don't understand what the appropriate response should be in these circumstances.

Chapter 5

Why People Fail Treatment

Although there are treatments for bipolar disorder, including medication and counseling, many people simply refuse to use them. They halt. They surrender. Simply put, they find it intolerable to battle both their bodies and brains. Simply put, they quit. This is not the ideal course of action for you to pursue when it comes to taking care of your ailment, as you can surely guess. However, a sizable portion of people with bipolar disorder will go through this emotion at some point.

How come? Antipsychotics and mood stabilizers are frequently the drug classes with the most negative effects and, consequently, the ones that patients discontinue taking the most frequently. However, those who abruptly stop using these medications without their doctor's advice frequently encounter serious problems. They experience a symptom relapse. They visit hospitals a lot. They become homeless, victims, and even more frequently take part in different sorts of crime. Those who lack the necessary prescriptions wind themselves in difficulty, either in jail or a hospital.

Noncompliance, or nonadherence, is the term used when a patient quits taking their prescription. This issue affects more people than only those who have bipolar disorder and use these medications. In reality, people who are told they must take drugs for a long time frequently go through a phase in which they no longer desire to do so.

Patients with epilepsy, hypertension, and even asthma frequently have this urge to quit taking their medications. It's important to realize that facing an issue doesn't necessarily need stopping all of your drugs. Some people only cease taking some of them—possibly the ones for which they still have pills on hand—while continuing to take others. Just as dangerous as individuals who must stop taking all of their drugs is partial disobedience. However, this doesn't provide a reason for why this occurs. Unfortunately, there are a variety of causes for why it will occur.

The primary and most frequent cause of this is that people don't comprehend the sickness they are dealing with. Ten out of every fourteen patients will quit taking their prescriptions because they are unaware of how crucial they are to their sickness.

Up to 80% of individuals only take their prescribed drugs as directed by their doctors. Many people only take their drugs as directed by their doctors without understanding why they need to. Because of this, it is challenging to gauge how conscious someone is of their sickness. Therefore, one of the most crucial things you can do is to fully comprehend your situation. Help your loved one stay educated about their illness if they have bipolar disorder. You must provide them with this information because if you don't, they might not understand how important it is to take those medications every day. However, protection from these issues may be significant with this education.

Chapter 6

How to Recognize Bipolar Symptoms & their Importance

Manic-depressive disease, another name for bipolar disorder, can have devastating effects on both the sufferer and those around them. The patient needs ongoing care from their treating psychiatrist, as well as from close friends and relatives. About two million Americans have been given a bipolar illness diagnosis. However, the majority of them are ignorant of the issue. In the majority of instances, symptoms start to manifest throughout adolescence or early adulthood. There is no need to be concerned because bipolar disorder is a manageable condition. To receive the right care after a diagnosis, people must be able to identify the various symptoms. People who suffer from bipolar disorder do not necessarily experience sadness or depression. They experience severe highs and lows in their moods, and it can be challenging to predict these mood swings. The patient frequently finds it challenging to handle unpredictable mood fluctuations. Always assume the worst while dealing with these patients because they occasionally commit themselves. Suicide, in their opinion, is the only way to combat this illness. In situations like this, dialing 911 is crucial.

To create and maintain the sufferer's strong support network, lifelong treatments, and drugs are required. Though, learning the fundamentals of how to detect the disorder's signs is the first step toward success.

Five Symptoms and Signs of Bipolar Disorder You Shouldn't Ignore

1. Manic episodes are simple to recognize. The boost in energy and

upbeat attitude are the most obvious factors. The beginning phases show this. After a prolonged period of depression, it is easy to spot when the patient suddenly becomes joyful and enthusiastic.
Other indicators include the need to go on expensive shopping sprees, concentration problems, and a rise in sexual desire.

2. Depression is simple to recognize but can be mistaken for a terrible day. Bipolar disorder is present if the depression persists for a significant amount of time. Bipolar disorder can be identified by a person's lack of interest in activities they once found enjoyable, such as hobbies and games.

3. Mood swings can manifest as psychosis symptoms including hallucinations or delusions in severe bipolar instances. Even though the patient may not be aware of this symptom, those around him can quickly identify it.

4. When a patient is in a mixed condition, it indicates they are experiencing both

mania and depression simultaneously. Lack of sleep, irritability, and changes in appetite might result from this. Those who have this form of bipolar disorder may experience great levels of energy yet still experience depression.

5). The most frightening and severe aspect of bipolar disorder is its morbid ideas. Most individuals tend to ignore this in the hope that it will go away if they do. When suicide seems likely, call 911 right away to prevent the worst from happening.

It is crucial to understand and remember that recognizing the symptoms of this illness can help identify its genuine nature. An incorrect diagnosis, or rather no diagnosis, implies the patient will continue to experience severe episodes and may eventually commit suicide. Even if they visit a doctor for their depression, the person might not discuss the mania portion of the disease. Recall that bipolar is a crippling illness that can be treated to lead a fulfilling and healthy life.

How Symptoms of Bipolar in Children Aid in Proper Diagnosis

Do you remember the date of the birth of your son or daughter? Do you recall counting each of his or her little fingers and toes at that time? When they reach adolescence, they start acting out of control. This is what? Who is this and where are they from? You bring him to the doctor, where you receive the bad news.

Your kid suffers from bipolar disorder. True, it's not a sentence to death. Nevertheless, it is still irritating. Bipolar Disorder is a serious and treatable condition. Extreme swings in energy, mood, behavior, and thought patterns serve as warning signs. Believe it or not, the person who was once your child has always been that child. According to doctors who specialize in bipolar disorders, it can even manifest in infancy and even the early years of life. ADHD is more frequently present in bipolar children. (Attention Deficit Hyperactivity Disorder).

In addition, parents are yearning for assistance and knowledge given everything that is going on. According to studies, 3.4 million adolescents or young adults who are depressed are experiencing the early stages of bipolar disorder even though the manic phase is never felt. Energy levels and moods fluctuate in youngsters with bipolar illnesses. Additionally, they exhibit severe agitation or experience elation from the tremendous energy spike.

Depression is characterized by extended periods of irritation or melancholy that are followed by low energy. Remember that the way the disease affects adults and children differs. Due to their hormonal makeup, youngsters are more likely to have continuous mood abnormalities, including episodes of depression and mania. It shifts quickly, causing many people to become chronically agitated.

Some Warning Symptoms of Bipolar Disorder

- Lack of playfulness

- Prolonged, explosive, and destructive rages
- Separation phobia
- Agitation related to bedwetting
- Sleep disorders
- Deep sadness
- Persistent desires for unhealthy foods like sugar or carbs
- Risk-taking behavior
- Illusions
- Not getting enough or too much sleep and
- Excessive trust in anything that defies laws or logic.

Parents stated that bipolar toddlers would have tremendous temper tantrums when they heard the word "NO." Save your lives by saying "no" to even the obvious solutions. Bipolar disorder in children can be brought on by a traumatic incident that causes either a manic high or manic depression. Later, when kids are agitated, the episodes may occur on their own. A significant risk factor for the condition is puberty, particularly when girls start their menstrual cycle.

According to studies, if parents fail to address their child's problem, it may take another 10 years before anything is done to stop the disorder from interfering with life. If there appear to be four or more symptoms, the child and parents should get evaluated. Teens with this illness who are not treated may turn to drugs and alcohol. Teenagers who appeared "normal" until recently and are now abruptly developing the disease are also more likely to use drugs and drink.

The condition is influenced by both genetic and environmental factors. Children that get early preventative measures or treatments have the capacity and potential to recover, achieve stability, and lead "normal" childhoods. Adverse effects are significantly decreased with appropriate and effective therapy. Investigations into the characteristics of children with the ailment are still ongoing. According to reviews so far, it is safe and effective for both children and adults.

Chapter 7

What to Do If Diagnosed with Bipolar Disorder

When a person is diagnosed with a sickness, a battle to treat it begins. After a formal diagnosis of a condition—be it cancer, AIDS, asthma, or something related to psychiatric problems like schizophrenia and bipolar disorder—there is usually some sort of battle going on. When the main symptoms of bipolar start to manifest, it is one of the mental disorders that people are forced to live with and attempt to manage. Essentially, they are fighting for their lives to return to normalcy. Every element of their lives may be affected, upsetting not just them but also everyone around them. Those who have the disease must be aware of any changes in behavior, if at all feasible! The indications are always present from the start, that they were made in the first place. Some of the intense manic highs and lows that are frequently seen with the disorder can be avoided with early therapy.

Early diagnosis of the illness increases the likelihood that treatment will be effective and decreases the likelihood of developing severe symptoms. The main challenge in caring for someone with this illness is motivating them to continue taking their medicine and attending talk therapy sessions.

Gaining their acceptance of responsibility is crucial to our ability to control the condition. Making some people understand that the diagnosis is accurate can be challenging since they don't want to accept that sickness is mostly to blame for their behavior. Others may feel as though a weight has been lifted off their shoulders as a result of learning that there are remedies available for what has been occurring to them.

Knowing that much of what was said and done could not have been prevented makes them happy, in their opinion. Even so, living with the past isn't any easier as a result. These are the people who believe they must continue taking their prescriptions. They are more inclined to seek assistance when something is hurting them. They are the ones that desire a life free from illness.

These people will consult their physician if anything doesn't look right. When they believe the initial diagnosis hasn't adequately helped them, many individuals will also seek a second opinion. The patient must have talk therapy in addition to medicines. Most doctors will advise this kind of treatment. Patients may not want to discuss their problems with a therapist. The patient's sickness is helped by chatting with a therapist, but the reality is.
As long as they intentionally remember to do it, a person with bipolar disorder can still take care of themselves regularly. Even though taking care of ourselves may seem straightforward,

bipolar patients must constantly remind themselves to do it. Some people with this illness can leave more active and, strangely enough, tranquil lives.

Despite all the medication and talk therapy they receive, it's healthier for them because if they hadn't received the diagnosis, they would have believed that the end of the world would be the solution.

Chapter 8

How to Properly Manage Bipolar Disorder Without Complications

One of the most important lessons you should take away from this book is that changing your lifestyle can help you get healthier. Bipolar disorder is something you can learn to manage. You might be sitting there contemplating how much you want to avoid dealing with this. You might wish to have the option of dismissing it with an "Oh well." However, you've already seen the justifications for why you can. Now that you're aware of that, take some time to consider what adjustments you may make to your lifestyle to truly raise your standard of living.

Not all of these adjustments should be attempted today. Allow yourself to work through each one with patience and time. By doing this, you will increase your capacity to successfully manage your bipolar condition. Unbelievably, your bipolar disorder is significantly influenced by the way you sleep. It's crucial to keep in mind that when you sleep in a regular pattern, chemical changes occur in the brain that are advantageous to your health. Simply getting enough sleep each night will help this problem, but make sure you do so by going to bed and waking up at roughly the same times every day.

Your bipolar symptoms will improve by developing a pattern like this. If your job requires you to sleep at odd hours of the day, you should strive to devise a plan that will ensure that you continue to do so even when you are not working. Your ability to cope depends on this. Additionally, it allows your mind the necessary time to relax and wake up feeling renewed. In reality, if you do need to move to a different time zone or make any significant adjustments to your sleep schedule, see your doctor about the best method to do so without endangering your health. We've covered the benefits of taking your prescribed drugs in great detail. But you can also develop coping skills to make this process even more beneficial for you. Even if you feel fantastic, take your meds. Even if you are symptom-free, follow your doctor's instructions for taking them.

Even if you feel fantastic, your medication is still at work! By ceasing to consume them, you are merely allowing the symptoms to reappear. Plan your calendar to include your dose to make the entire medication-taking process simple.

For instance, eat breakfast and take your morning medications as soon as you wake up. If you need to take another tablet later on in the day, do so, for instance, after dinner. You can prevent forgetting to take your medications, for example, by taking them with meals.

Why Support Groups are Important for Bipolar Patients

Everyone despises groups, and nobody wants to attend any. But consider why that might be. Is it too difficult for you to perform? Do you find it difficult to admit that something might be off? Perhaps you are one of the many people who struggle with the need to surround yourself with people who experience the same difficulties as you do.

Overall, support groups can help you improve your quality of life and become more aware of the challenges you are facing. Being able to manage bipolar disorder is difficult but not impossible. You can discover how to do it.

Working with people who are in similar positions to you is perhaps one of the finest methods to do this. Support groups provide that kind of care, which neither your family nor friends nor your doctor can provide for you. Being with people who are going through similar issues as you do gives you hope, understanding, and sometimes even a sense of serenity.

Finding out about support groups is crucial. Who is in yours depends on the composition of your family as well as the people who are making an effort to give you the care you require. You most likely have a family that is now providing for your needs. Additionally, the medical staff is there to help you with any medical needs.

This applies to everyone, from your primary care physician to the psychiatrist you've confided in deeply. You should include your friends in your support system. Many people are reluctant to disclose personal information, such as their bipolar disease, but you should.

A good friend stands by you, aids in your adjustment, and provides you with the support you require at all times. Think about telling your loved ones what is going on. You can only gain from it. Additionally, it might make you a greater friend to them by enabling them to comprehend your reactions and mood swings.

While having your family close by will enhance your well-being and provide the assistance you require, you should also think about getting additional support from outside support groups. Bipolar disorder support groups for professionals can be available at numerous hospitals, recreation centers, and mental facilities.

Ask your doctor for recommendations so you can locate one close to you. Depending on your circumstances, they might have one ready for you to choose from that is tailored to your particular needs. These support organizations offer qualified assistance that you can direct.

For instance, a moderator can bring together numerous people who share your disorder. People benefit from hearing about the details of your day just as much as you benefit from doing the same for yourself.

What You Should Know & Do About Your Child's Bipolar Disorder

Most parents show their children that they care straight away. Parents worry endlessly over even the smallest sneeze when their child is a baby. Parents frequently worry about their children. Parents should never stop worrying about their kids' well-being, both physically and emotionally.

Children show signs of abnormalities even at a young age, and while childhood development has a role in that, it is now believed that some brain illnesses start in childhood and worsen as children get older. Parents must be aware of their children's level of activity. Many people are suffering from Bipolar conditions today, which is a sort of mental or brain condition. This illness may have an impact on a person's social interactions as well as daily tasks and activities.

When a child is affected, it has a significant impact on their academic achievement, interactions with other children, and even their connections with their parents and siblings. Severe mood swings or shifts can be brought on by bipolar disorder. It is also known as manic depression.

When a child is younger, parents may find it slightly simpler to identify the disease's symptoms. When a child has bipolar disorder, they will alternate between periods of uncharacteristically great happiness and intense sadness or depression. For kids, it all happens in a split second. In young people, the disease's symptoms are typically noticeable.

Studies have shown that young children can and do exhibit these symptoms as well, but because their parents may not be familiar with this illness, they may overlook the "warning" indications. Most parents believe that their child's behavior as they mature is typical of this process. However, ignoring the warning signs can harm a person's everyday life and seriously damage their relationships with their parents, siblings, and friends.

Common Bipolar Disorder Symptoms in Children.

- Excessive joy
- I'm too downcast
- Enhanced energy

- Sleep loss
- Irritable enough
- Quick-witted
- Exaggerated confidence in one's abilities and talents
- Deficient judgment; and
- Aggressive conduct

As you can see, it is quite challenging to identify bipolar children. Some parents believe the behavior to be typical and believe that the symptoms will pass as the kids get older. Keep an eye on your child's behavior and mood if you have any suspicions. There is a chance they could be bipolar if they change abruptly.

Consult your child's doctor as soon as you can so that they can suggest a fantastic psychiatrist. This physician will be able to diagnose your child and begin a course of therapy that is suitable for both your family and them. A bipolar mood can be stabilized with medication.

The youngster must get care since the longer the illness goes undiagnosed, the more difficult it is for the family and the patient.

All of these could potentially result in a suicide attempt. Diagnosing bipolar disorder early is essential for effective therapy. Keep an eye out for any odd behavior in kids, and if anything appears off, visit your pediatrician. Parents may be confident that their child will receive all the assistance necessary to grow up normally and contribute positively to society with the right care and support.

Chapter 9

Bipolar Disorder Treatment Options for Children

The bipolar disease was once thought to solely affect adults, but research has shown that kids can also develop manic-depressive illness. One problem is that many children are given the diagnosis of attention deficit disorder (ADD) and attention deficit hyperactivity disorder (ADHD), even though bipolar is increasingly being recognized in children and adolescents by researchers and medical professionals. Children who receive diagnoses early have a better chance of receiving effective therapy and leading restricted lives rather than chaotic ones. However, it appears like there is debate surrounding anything having to do with kids. There are issues with treating bipolar in youngsters with medication. Many doctors believe that talk therapy combined with medicine, which is always given initially, will be effective. Many parents and psychologists, nevertheless, are against this approach.

It appears that children lose some of their personality as soon as parents become aware that their child is on medicine. Parents' apparent love for their sense of self. In reality, that is not true. When someone is medicated, even excessively medicated, they never lose their sense of self.

However, some youngsters may indeed become "spacey" or just "out of it" when taking certain drugs. Naturally, this raises concerns among the parents and the medical community, prompting them to wonder whether the child would be healthier without medication and whether it is indeed required. Play therapy is a successful treatment for kids, especially for kids with bipolar disorder. These kids typically have happier childhoods. In play therapy, the child is frequently put in hypothetical circumstances where they must come up with an emotionally and cognitively sound response.

For some children, play therapy is beneficial, but not for others. Some bipolar kids experience mood swings that are so extreme that lose control over both their emotional responses and other behavior in different contexts. The introduction of Cognitive Behavioral Therapy is a novel therapy.

The focus of therapy Is helping the patient identify the symptoms of bipolar disorder, their causes, and the inappropriate behaviors that go along with them. It also suggests substitutes for that "bad" behavior.

Through this therapy, the patient can learn for themselves how to successfully regulate and prevent manic or depressed episodes. This is an excellent alternative for adults, but it's still very new for kids. This treatment does complement medical treatment well.

Children often do not resolve crises or engage in critical thinking, but cognitive therapy does. Due to these restrictions on age and maturity, it is rarely utilized with young children. According to some studies, cognitive and behavioral therapy would be effective if it were modified and tailored toward children.

However, doing so can be challenging. Children's treatment alternatives should be addressed with their doctor, psychiatrists, psychologists, parents, and teachers to come up with a manageable and practical course of action, regardless of the outcome.

For the process to be successful, every person the child interacts with needs to be aware of it. They must speak up when necessary if they have worries about the child's potential impacts or notice a difference in a negative outcome. If parents believe their child is not receiving the care and attention they require, they should not hesitate to switch doctors. Treatment aims to help the youngster live in society and behave "normally," as required by law.

Chapter 10

Bipolar Disorder Treatments

It's not unusual for someone with bipolar disorder to go for close to eight years without receiving a diagnosis. Despite the availability of effective medicines, they continue to go undetected or receive subpar care. If the sickness is not addressed, it may have a variety of negative effects on the person's life. As soon as symptoms appear, a diagnosis must be made so that treatment can begin. There are several treatments available for bipolar disorder, and while some may be unsuccessful, others have had great success in managing the illness. Patients may tend to stop taking their medications because they believe they are just not functioning.

This could be risky because a medication slip could result in a recurrence of episodes. Another aspect of treating the condition is compliance.

Stages of Treatment

- Acute and preventive care

The goal of the acute stage is to stop any existing manic, hypomanic, mixed, and depressive symptoms. To handle future incidents, preventative steps necessitate continuing the therapy process. Treatment can take the form of medication, psychotherapy, or instruction. All patients must receive medication therapy during both phases. During psychotherapy sessions, patients and families often find relief from symptoms of bipolar disorder that are more severe than typical.

Families and patients must be informed of the signs of this condition and how to treat it due to its complexity. It's crucial to raise awareness of this illness so that people can prepare for it. Regardless of the course of therapy selected by the patient, their family, and their doctor, the fundamental objective is to lessen the number of episodes that the bipolar person experiences and stop it from cycling through each mood stage. It would be advantageous if the mood disturbances become less severe and less frequent. The patient would benefit from this even while they are between bouts.

Before prescribing any medication or other forms of treatment, the doctor must first determine what triggered the original outburst during talk therapy. The doctor will then check for any additional issues, such as emotional or medical ones, that can obstruct the patient's therapy and recovery.

Treatment Options

Bipolar people can benefit from several drugs in their day-to-day life.

- Mood stabilizers

The basis of medical treatment for bipolar disorder is this. Even in the most severe episodes of psychotic mania, they are effective. It can also be used as a medication for maintenance. Lithium and Valproate are the two medicines that are most frequently administered in this region. The medications have a stimulating effect.

- Antipsychotic Drug

This mood stabilizer is also approved for use in schizophrenia treatment. This treatment uses five different types of drugs. Bipolar mania and mixed episodes can be treated with olanzapine, risperidone, quetiapine, ziprasidone, and, among other medications. For mixed episodes, only quetiapine is permitted, nevertheless. The nice part about the medications is that they can be taken either alone or in conjunction with other medications to assist treat disease symptoms.

- Antiseizure drugs

Patients with rapid bipolar cycling, mixed periods of mania and depression, and those who have abused substances frequently receive this treatment. Carbamazepine, lamotrigine, and oxcarbazepine are the three anti-seizure medications prescribed.

- Electroconvulsive treatment: ordered for individuals who are experiencing severe emotional distress.

- Sleep Management and Psychotherapy

Used with bipolar disorder medicines. The drug has side effects, just like any other product. Some of these include diabetes, elevated cholesterol, and weight gain. A diet should be adhered to, and knowledge of dietary intake is essential. This may aid in minimizing these effects. The patient can lead a "normal" life if they have friends and family supporting them.

- Pharmaceutical Treatment

This kind of therapy includes the use of medication. They are used to manage irrational behavior and mood fluctuations brought on by mania and depression. A few medications can also aid in reducing severe panic episodes. There are five different categories into which treatment falls in this field. Sedatives and anti-anxiety medications: There are various kinds of sedatives. They typically offer the bipolar person some relief. It helps the patient receive the appropriate quantity of sleep he needs to get a good night's sleep. Additionally, it can be used to lessen anxiety and regulate manic episodes. Patients are typically given hypnotics, tranquilizers, anxiolytics, and benzodiazepines, among other well-known drugs.

Chapter 11

Long-Term Bipolar Disorder Treatment

Bipolar disorder has been identified in a large number of people worldwide, and these people are affected by it. However, there are still a great number of undiagnosed cases. It must be noted that the condition might worsen the longer it remains undetected. Therefore, those who suspect they have the condition should visit a doctor right away to receive care and medication. People who have this illness could believe that everything is normal. However, it would have a significant impact on their family and friends. This is the reason visiting a doctor is so crucial. They can give prescriptions for drugs that can manage and treat bipolar disorder symptoms. The Federal Treatment and Administration (FDA) has approved a long-term treatment named Lamictal in contrast to the majority of bipolar illness medications, which only provide temporary relief. Adults with Bipolar 1 symptoms should take Lamictal. Studies have demonstrated that the medication can avoid mood swings for a longer amount of time. If this drug is suitable for you or not can be determined by your doctor.

This medicine may be helpful for some people because long-term trials demonstrate that it prevents mood changes until the episodes require extra therapy. Since depression can stay the longest, medication has been very successful in preventing it from occurring. 18 months has been the lengthiest delayed effect.

- Lamictal Adverse Reactions

This medication won't be provided to all patients. The medication may cause headaches, dizziness, double or blurred vision, tiredness, nausea, poor coordination, vomiting, rash, and insomnia in patients who take it. Some people may get an uncommon skin side reaction that necessitates.

Children are the ones who exhibit this most frequently. For patients who are at least 18 years old, this is conventional treatment. Lamictal is widely used, however, its efficacy has not yet been shown. You will discuss the medication's suitability for you with your doctor before you begin using it. Patients can follow the prescription label more easily thanks to kits that are readily available. Take the medication exactly as directed for the best results.

It is Important to Note the Following

- You can take Lamictal before any occurrences.
- The dosage will be started at a lower level and raised progressively over time.
- Patients should consult their doctor if they have any negative effects.

- You can begin to anticipate experiencing the full impact of the medication within a few weeks.

A patient should visit the hospital right away if they have strange thoughts. When purchasing Lamictal, ensure that the prescription is for the appropriate drug. The improper medication can result in very serious issues. Keep in mind to read and examine the labels carefully.

Make careful to stick to the strategy you and your doctor created. Any prescribed drug falls within this category. Bipolar disorder is a chronic condition that a sufferer must comprehend. They will have to live with this illness for the rest of their lives. They ought to comprehend that. If your doctor has not instructed you to stop taking your medication, do not.

Additionally, record your symptoms and keep a journal to show your doctor. This will aid him or her in determining whether you should keep taking Lamictal. Keep a log of your moods and sleep as well. Lamictal should be used to control allergic responses. If you're a woman and considering getting pregnant or are already pregnant, consult your doctor first. Any drug should help you have a "normal" life.

Chapter 12

Difference Between Childhood Bipolar and Asperger's Syndrome

Due to the similarity of their symptoms, pediatric bipolar disorder and Asperger's disorder are treated in very similar ways. But what are these two ailments specifically, and how are they similar? Manic depression, also referred to as pediatric bipolar disorder, is a condition that can manifest as mood swings or mood cycling. Pediatric type one patients frequently have periods of mania followed by depressive spells. Pediatric type two patients endure alternating spells of mania and deep depression. Asperger's disorder is thought to be a milder version of autism and is related to it. It's a sort of pervasive developmental disease that affects growth, particularly in terms of social and communication skills. What symptoms of mania and depression are present in bipolar disorder? Anger, intense melancholy, excessive sleep, and thoughts of worthlessness are all indications of depression.

Rage, intense happiness, increased energy, hyperactivity, distractibility, insufficient sleep, and obsessive behaviors are all indications of mania. There are four distinct causes of the disease. Neurological, biological, emotional, and environmental are them. However, not all of these elements will be present in every instance. Since there is currently little knowledge regarding the illness, progress is still being done in this area.

Symptoms of Asperger's Syndrome

Social skill issues, unusual or repetitive actions, communication problems, and a narrow range of interests are all signs of this illness.

Although the exact causes of Asperger's disorder are unknown, research has indicated that the condition is inherited because it does run in families. This must imply that the illness is biological, which implies that it is either genetic or neurologically connected. There aren't any solutions to this question as of yet.

Bipolar Disorder and Asperger's Syndrome Share Certain Similarities:

Asperger's disorder and pediatric bipolar disorder are quite similar and can result in a misdiagnosis because of this. Odd behaviors, compulsive behavior, and wrath episodes are similar signs. Both illnesses frequently exhibit behavioral, educational, and anger concerns as well as a lack of social development abilities.

Asperger's disorder and bipolar disorder can coexist, and this is most frequently the case. However, it is unclear if the chemical imbalances assumed to be the root of pediatric bipolar illness are connected to the neurological repercussions that create Asperger's disorder. Some solutions to the sickness should become available as medical research into neurological, technological, and mental difficulties progresses.

Treatments Behind Asperger's Disorder and Bipolar Disorder Diseases

There are medications to address the symptoms of both conditions, but there are no medications specifically for Asperger's Disorder. Asperger's symptoms are remarkably similar to those of bipolar disorder, hence Asperger's drugs can also be utilized for bipolar.

Both Asperger syndrome and bipolar disorder are treated with counseling in addition to medication. While counseling is necessary so people can learn to deal with their condition, the majority of Asperger's patients do not receive medication. If you are aware of a child displaying any of the aforementioned behaviors, you should take them as soon as possible to the doctor so they can be diagnosed.

A course of action for therapy can be created after a diagnosis has been made. Any untreated disorders in either party might cause serious issues for the affected child's friends, family, and community.

Chapter 13

How to Love Someone with Bipolar Disorder

Giving someone with bipolar disease unconditional love might be challenging. They will avoid you because it is never easy for them to show their love. Assisting those who may see themselves highly is difficult for those who are rejected. However, caring for and appreciating someone who has been diagnosed with this illness, someone with confused thoughts and manners, is never simple. People must learn everything there is to know about the sickness. If you don't find out what is going on with the person you love, you won't know what they are going through.

After reading the explanation and learning associations with the condition, it should be time to develop a strategy that will aid you in resolving any issues.

- Recognize the disease's symptoms first

Your fault is not in this. It is never your fault that your loved one has the condition or behaves the way they do. He or she won't be able to direct their behavior. When parents with young children receive a diagnosis, it may be particularly difficult for them to comprehend. Recognize the signs of the disorder and learn to identify them. Has the person ever had trouble sleeping? Keep an eye on his attitude, deeds, and reactions to others. So that you can remember when and where it happened, note it down. Be not ashamed of the illness, especially when its symptoms are manifesting.

- Do not interpret the disorder as a personal slight from you.

When you love someone, you accept them as they are, disease and all. You can look past it. It is not a condition that can be treated, then recurs. Treating it as pervasive is better for the loved one because it is. Just keep in mind that the ailment cannot be healed by luxury. You are not assisting him in getting better and are allowing him to be worse off than he already is if you feel ashamed of his condition.

- Learn to trust

Getting acclimated to the illness involves learning to trust people. They want you to convince them rather than handing them off to someone else's trust or care. There are moments when it seems impossible to love your loved one and you are tempted to call the police or a doctor because you no longer want to take care of them. Never utter the phrases in their hearing range. It causes more harm than good and is certain to make things worse.

- Maintain clear and honest lines of communication.

Keep it open at all times, and be prepared to lend an ear if they need it. After acknowledging the symptoms, consider what you can do to help even though certain seemingly helpful actions may not be so. Here, communication is effective. Do not repress your emotions. There are constructive ways to express your feelings without hurting the other person. Avoid nagging, preaching, or lecturing because these behaviors may make them want to distance themselves from you.

- Positive encouragement will help. Be comforting and gentle. Serving your loved one could limit what he or she is capable of, so avoid doing so. Let him come up with answers to the issues he perceives for himself. Allow him to live his own life. If he does, he will feel better about himself. Above everything else, show him or her your support, love, and understanding.

Some Scenarios of Bipolar Disorder Symptom

Could you explain bipolar disorder to someone right now without making them feel perplexed? Almost always, bipolar disorder is connected to mood swings between mania and depression. This isn't always the case, though. The ability to bend time in ways that Einstein could not have imagined is, in fact, the primary symptom and feature of this disease. Situations involving bipolar disorder are comparable to stop lights when automobiles are backed up and stuck. The world seems to be moving slowly, and everyone is only interested in making you happy. If someone takes advantage of you, you could become angry at them occasionally and feel upset.

In the beginning, you might come across vehicles that let you weave in and out of traffic. Then, due to their extreme stickiness and proximity to one another, some cars might not even let you through. You'll eventually become so stuck that you'll finally smack your head against the dashboard in utter panic, desperate to escape yet unable to. Then, things can be turned around. You could remain motionless while standing still.

Then, because your mind is preoccupied with that task, it becomes impossible to move to another one. It is comparable to waiting till the water in the shower runs cold before doing anything else. Sometimes when you wake up it seems impossible to leave your bed. A bipolar individual can react and generate more quickly. Imagine that you are the batter facing the pitcher. Visualize the ball coming toward you. From there, you can immediately predict the ball's course.

Once the ball is coming your way, you can give it a solid whack with the bat. Even these things, though, change with time. The clock will undoubtedly go faster or slower. You might swing at the ball a little bit too early when you're in quick mode, but by repeatedly doing it, you can get used to missing bats.

You lose your cool because you think the ball is taking an eternity to reach you, even though it isn't. Now you concentrate on your wrath and vent it on the bat, the ground, or possibly the person who is now closest to you. Everything appears to be going wrong. That's what your mind is telling you, at least. Everyone, including God, has turned against you. Even computers are putting up barriers and coming up with new mathematical techniques to keep you down. You start to cry because the situation is too much for you to handle. You never forget those stillnesses, those minutes spent in the shower and on the bed.

You can even recall when you were energetic. Everything was and still is conceivable in your head. There isn't enough room in space to accomplish what you wished to. You could explore a new universe that you owned where everything may change.

Instead of bipolar disorder or manic depression, chronicity may be responsible for the symptoms mentioned. This kind of person can go through a wide range of experiences, from extreme speed to total stillness.

Some days are more hyperactive than others when it comes to activities. You can start a big project and abandon it the next. Bipolar disorder is treatable with medication and talk therapy, regardless of how bad it may seem.

The patient must cooperate throughout the drawn-out, slow process.

Chapter 14

Bipolar Disorder vs. Schizophrenia

Treatments for these conditions are currently available and are effective in managing schizophrenia and bipolar disorder. To manage the disorders, psychotherapy, and drugs that alter the chemistry of the brain are both quite effective. The consequences of the signs and symptoms are lessened as a result of the medications and talk therapy sessions helping to stabilize brain processes. Keep in mind that schizophrenia and bipolar disorder have extremely similar outward symptoms, making it easy for even a doctor to mistake one for the other. When a patient has two diseases, medications for one of them won't function. At this point, the patient should discuss the problem with the doctor. If he or she is unable to discuss it, a trustworthy family member should. Clozaril is one of the more well-liked medications provided to people with schizophrenia. It was made specifically for those with schizophrenia, and bipolar patients should never take it. It's meant to help people regain control of their brain activity. Lithium, a powerful medication that prevents recurrent manic episodes in bipolar disorder patients, is frequently recommended.

Valproic acid is frequently prescribed by specialists to people with fast-cycling bipolar disorder. This may also benefit bipolar patients who cycle frequently. It is crucial that a patient with any of these two diseases, or a loved one who has one of them, find a physician they can trust to look after them. In the sphere of mental diseases, they must be widely acknowledged. The patient will receive the proper sort of care required for their recovery, as well as medications to speed it up, by selecting the right doctor. Early diagnosis of bipolar disorder and schizophrenia is crucial for effective therapy. It is important to get treated as soon as you or someone else detects something because these two mental illnesses can ruin your life and render you an "unproductive" member of society. If not, it will deteriorate over time and have a significant impact on how you live, work, and interact with others and the outside world.

- Power levels

The disease's energy level is the most obvious modification. Depression results in a person having low energy and feeling exhausted. They could even appear to respond slowly. Energy levels are through the roof and they engage in greater quantities of activities when they are experiencing the manic side of the illness.

- Self-esteem problems

Self-esteem problems are also common. In mania, the person becomes irresponsible because they believe they are high and powerful, whereas a depressed person feels guilty and believes they are unworthy. This occasionally makes the person unsure about what to do. Because of the underlying themes, depression and manic symptoms of the disorder substantially differ from one another. Depression is characterized by slowness, dullness, smallness, introversion, and hopelessness. Mania symptoms can cause things to seem exaggerated, large, quick, extroverted, and full of impossibly optimistic dreams.

- Varying concentrations

On the surface, it would appear that bipolar symptoms are closely related. Because mania is characterized by hyperactivity and depression by low concentration, both conditions can be viewed as having similar degrees of concentration. Both struggle with their internal thoughts. The sole distinction is that a depressed person has fewer thoughts, whereas a manic person has rapid ideas.

- Sleeping habits

For both sorts of patients, even sleep cycles are disturbed. They may experience major troubles as a result of their life. Depression makes it so that the sufferer doesn't care whether they sleep or not. When they do sleep, it will be for extended periods.

When they don't get any rest, it may take them some time to crash. The less sleep a person with mania needs, the better they feel, in their opinion. These patients may go for days without taking a break. Because this disease's symptoms can manifest in both extremes, both forms are of particular concern. When depressed, a person is inclined to consider suicide or death, and may even make plans to end their life.

However, a person with manic symptoms may have ideas about delusions and strange perceptions involving both aural and visual illusions. If someone has bipolar disorder, they will experience some, all, or almost all of the symptoms from both ends of the spectrum. Individuals or the people they love in their lives must become aware of the symptoms and seek treatment as soon as possible because this sickness can be serious and have life-altering effects.

Chapter 15

How to be Successful Despite Having Bipolar

Being intelligent and in good health is necessary for success in life. The central processing unit of our body, the brain, must be flawless for us to have a happy and successful life, although any physical limitations of the body can be overcome. We need a sharp mind for all of our errands to comprehend our surroundings, act quickly, and make well-considered decisions. We also need to have control over our emotions in addition to a brain that functions correctly. Being excessively happy or furious all the time would not be of any benefit to us. To use the proper phrase, all of our psychological components must be sufficiently balanced. What happens if you find out that you or someone you know has a brain disorder? Bipolar disorder is one of these widespread brain disorders. In severe circumstances, this illness can cause suicides in addition to having an impact on our emotions and daily actions.

6 Facts you should know

1. People who have bipolar disorder frequently liken their lives to roller coasters. Their life is filled with tremendous highs and terrible lows.

2. even though there is no known effective treatment for this disease, there are several techniques to manage its progression and mood swings. Many people have benefited from these techniques and have had longer, healthier lives.

3. If you constantly struggle to complete tasks satisfactorily, feel as though your mind is becoming dull and that you are essentially useless, no longer find humor amusing, or have become uncontrollably

agitated, irritable, scared, or angry, you may be suffering from bipolar disorder.

4. Excessive shyness, tremendous desire for seduction and sexuality, and a strong sense of ease, strength, exhilaration, and omnipotence are some additional major signs of bipolar disorder.

5. Although many individuals believe these symptoms are only transient, it is always advisable to seek medical assistance.

6. To prevent any unfavorable and disastrous outcomes, such ailment must receive attention as soon as possible before it is too late. If you or a member of your family exhibits these signs, you must begin using therapeutic options rather than giving up and feeling helpless.

Chapter 16

10 Important Things to Note When Taking Medications for Bipolar Disorder

Being intelligent and in good health is necessary for success in life. The central processing unit of our body, the brain, must be flawless for us to have a happy and successful life, although any physical limitations of the body can be overcome. We need a sharp mind for all of our errands to comprehend our surroundings, act quickly, and make well-considered decisions. We also need to have control over our emotions in addition to a brain that functions correctly. Being excessively happy or furious all the time would not be of any benefit to us. To use the proper phrase, all of our psychological components must be sufficiently balanced. What happens if you find out that you or someone you know has a brain disorder? Bipolar disorder is one of these widespread brain disorders. In severe circumstances, this illness can cause suicides in addition to having an impact on our emotions and daily actions.

Medical professionals combine medicine with counseling or therapy to treat bipolar disorder. It is important to realize that other elements are beneficial and can control the disease before moving on to a chosen list of the medications recommended for bipolar disorder.

Instead, you must realize that while helpful, drugs are a somewhat haphazard form of therapy. All of these have adverse effects that must be disclosed to the doctor, who will then adjust the patient's prescription as soon as it is necessary.

Medications for bipolar disorder & Usage

1. Medication Types
The following drugs are frequently prescribed for bipolar disorder:

a. Mood stabilizer
b. Anti-psychotics
c. anxiety medications
d. antidepressants

2. How they are used
In addition to the therapy, doctors or psychiatrists frequently combine two or more of these drugs. These drugs significantly improve the patient's therapy's effectiveness.

3. Amoxapine or Asendin
This antidepressant is frequently recommended to treat clinical depression and bipolar disorder. Cottonmouth, sleepiness, nausea, headaches, dizziness, and increased hunger are among its more well-known side effects. Other, less frequent side effects exist as well. These include nausea, vomiting, increased perspiration, diarrhea, and heartburn.

4. Aventyl or Palemor
This antidepressant is another one that has been proven to be effective in treating bipolar depression. All of its side effects are comparable to those of amoxapine or asendin.

5. Bupropion, Wellbutrin, or Zyban
Perhaps the most frequently prescribed medication for people with bipolar disorder is this one. In terms of the purposes it fulfills, it is a well-known antidepressant, although structurally, it is unrelated to the antidepressant drug family. The medical community is still unsure of the precise reason why this medication is so effective in treating bipolar disorder.

6. Ativan
Patients with bipolar disorder can effectively address the symptoms of excessive anxiety with this anti-anxiety drug. Dizziness, unbalance, drowsiness, and slurred speech are some of its adverse effects. Abdominal pain, fuzzy vision, headache, cotton mouth, nausea, weakness, and shaking or shakiness are

less frequent adverse effects of this medication.

7. Klonopin

This well-known anti-anxiety medication has shown promising outcomes in the treatment of bipolar disorder patients. All of its side effects resemble those of Ativan.

8. Tegretol

This anti-seizure medication was later authorized for use as an anti-psychotic medication for people with bipolar illness. It is frequently prescribed instead of a mood stabilizer, particularly for people with bipolar I disorder. Its well-known side effects include drowsiness, nausea, trembling, and dizziness.

9. Depakote

This anti-seizure medication also works well to stabilize mood in people with bipolar disorder. Although the adverse effects are comparable to those of Tegretol, they can get rather bad in this situation. When it comes to mood stabilizers, Tegretol has recently taken the position of Depakote.

10. Verapamil is a calcium blocker that helps people with bipolar disorder who are experiencing mania. It belongs to the class of blood pressure medicines. Before now, medical professionals said that this drug had remarkable mood-stabilizing abilities. Due to its lack of effectiveness, its current use in people with bipolar illness is practically over.

Chapter 17

How To Treat Bipolar Disorder With CBT

Bipolar disorder, often known as manic depression, is a mental illness that can be brought on by a variety of reasons, including biological, neurological, environmental, and emotional ones. It is characterized by extremely frequent mood swings or cycling between intense emotions like mania and depression and the patient's typical behavior. Bipolar disorder can be treated in several ways, but the most popular approach is a mix of counseling and medication. But not every patient can be subjected to the same drill. Drug misuse histories mean that certain patients cannot be treated with medication since there is a high chance of adverse outcomes. It is also difficult to determine if mood swings are a result of bipolar disorder or pharmaceuticals, and it is safe to assume that if the patient did not already have a severe case of bipolar disorder, the medication would seriously hurt them. Another fundamental truth is that patients only turn to medication as a last resort.

CBT is introduced in such unique situations where drugs are not the best option. Cognitive Behavioral Therapy, sometimes known as CBT, is a type of therapy that helps patients identify the precise reasons and triggers of their manic and depressed moods.

The patients are then taught coping mechanisms to deal with the symptoms during episodes as well as methods to avoid triggers going forward. 70% of people with bipolar I illness are required to participate in CBT, particularly those who have experienced one or more episodes within four years after beginning CBT.

There are two main objectives of CBT for bipolar illness management. Which are:

i. Being aware of manic episodes before they spiral out of control and changing one's response to them consciously.
ii. To acquire the methods, ideas, feelings, and activities that would lessen their depression.

These objectives are successfully met via the use of the numerous exercises and methods advised by knowledgeable therapists. The effectiveness of CBT for treating bipolar disorder mostly depends on the patient, who is assigned homework that may include exercises, reading, and other activities.

These are geared at assisting the patient in comprehending their condition and in learning coping mechanisms.

How to Conduct CBT Treatment for Bipolar Disorder

- Making an Agreement with the Patient:

Before beginning CBT, you must agree on a therapy plan with your patient. In this treatment, you create a clear treatment plan for the patient, and they both agree to adhere to it. The patient's pledge to finish all of his schoolwork and treat all assignments seriously is also included in this. In this contract, the patient also promises to take all prescription medications exactly as instructed. This is an important step in CBT since the patient's motivation to manage bipolar disorder and sense of accountability for it are key components of the procedure.

- Capturing Mood Swings

The second stage of CBT is tracking and rating the patient's moods. For this, the doctor provides the patient with several worksheets to do regularly. The patient logs his or her daily feelings on these papers. They also keep track of other crucial information, such as how many hours they slept, their level of worry, and their level of irritation. Patients with Bipolar II Disorder in particular must keep daily records of all this information because their moods change drastically with   this   condition.

- The patient completes their homework

The next phase in CBT is for the patient once the therapist can comprehend the bipolar patient's mood cycles. Here, the therapist gives the patient some reading material to help them fully grasp how our thoughts influence our emotions.
The patient does this by completing worksheets, and once they have mastered the exercise, they can practice by changing their thinking more sensibly. The frequency and intensity of the manic and depressed episodes decrease as a result of their emotions becoming more reasonable.

- Identifying the Triggers:

Additionally, you must be able to identify the triggers of the condition you are treating. An emotional or physical trigger is essentially anything that sets off a manic or depressive episode, including feelings, ideas, seasons, circumstances, settings, events, etc.

Once the patient begins to recognize and comprehend their triggers, he or she will be able to learn to completely avoid them, hence reducing the severity and frequency of the manic and depressive episodes.

Overall, CBT is a very effective way of treatment for people with bipolar disorder. Before it's too late, speak with your doctor or therapist if you believe you need this therapy.

Conclusion

A Big Congratulations to you for making it to the point.

I hope these Strategies bring you lasting solution to the challenges faced as a result of this predicament...